Susan Fay West

Change Habits: ADHD Style

Susan Fay West
Coach & ADHD Specialist

Susan Fay West

Dedication

To Donna. You encourage me and believe in me to dream bigger.
"Bright, beautiful you."

Sound familiar?

*"Every single day is such a **struggle**. It's so hard to keep it all together."*

*"I don't know how to **prioritize**. Everything feels like it should be priority."*

*"I can't **get started**. And I can't put on the brakes once I DO get started."*

*"I'm tired of **forgetting** so many things."*

*"I'm tired of people thinking I don't **care**. At work and at home."*

It's a steep climb ….

Good for You for Being Here

This book is for you if you are ….

➢ Recently, officially diagnosed (Finally, you understand, right?). But now what?

➢ Diagnosed as a child or young adult, your ADHD was going along okay and now seems to have erupted like a volcano. This is fairly typical as life gets more complex.

➢ Transitioning into high school, college, married life, or building a family: these are all are "tipping points" when what used to work doesn't seem to anymore.

"Sue understands adult ADHD! Sue's breadth of knowledge really helped to sort out what does work - and much to my great relief - what does not work. Understanding how to create motivation, what saps it, and the conditions that I work best in is freeing and has been a real confidence-builder! "

➢ Perhaps you're a mid or later life woman, who has multiple roles, along with hormonal changes. These will make it difficult to keep up, "suddenly."

➢ Perhaps you're not officially diagnosed. But your friends, spouse and others are tired of (_fill in the blank for your own life_) and you have decided it is time. Time to figure it out because you want to feel better about yourself, you want to manage life more easily and follow through on your word.

I get it. I wrote this workbook to help you discover a new set of plays to manage your days and life more easily.

A normal part of the ADHD brain is that short term and working memory are not as strong as when ADHD is not in the mix. "Working" memory is how many things you can keep in mind at once. An example is keeping a list in your head. Knowing you have 6 items to get at the store, but forget several when you get into the store.

You've probably noticed that sometimes you have had a workable system but as time goes along, you forget about using the system. Or you change something because you think it's the system and change again and again … and then get lost in so many systems.

This workbook **gives you one place to keep track**. You'll also find education, tracking sheets, tips and client comments.

I hope other people's experience will inspire you to keep going and believe that the work you'll do will pay off. You'll see some of their words throughout the book.

Suggestions for Getting Started with the Workbook

Getting started IS difficult if you have or think you have ADHD, so I need to offer some getting started strategies to use with your workbook!

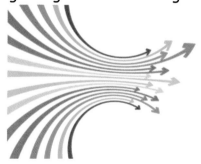

Open it. That's it.

- Open up to the table of contents; it's right after this getting started section. Leave it open. Read if you want or don't, but by leaving it open, it's a reminder.

- Or, open it AND read just a few pages. Use a 5-minute timer or Time Timer.

- Do it again, as you walk by the open book. Anytime you have 5 minutes.

- This is purely to get you into it, not to finish, or make any big decisions; a short way to get your mind engaged .... Because that's what the ADHD brain needs.

- When you decide to read, if starting at the beginning is too boring (common), then read the table of contents and choose a topic that looks kind of intriguing. Start there and let it lead you.

Make a date with yourself & the workbook/playbook.

- Do you have time alone at home? A favorite coffee shop? Take the workbook with you.

- Take an hour or two on a weekend. Make it a mini retreat.

Traveling? Take the workbook with you (or at least an exercise or two).

▪ A train or plane ride is like having a bubble of quiet time surrounding you.

▪ If you don't have that option, how could you create a "bubble" of quiet time? Put "blinders" on to avoid <u>distractions?</u>

Don't do anything …. call me to figure out where to get started.

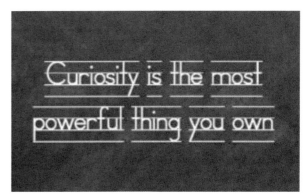

▪ With your purchase, you received a free 1/2 hour with me to get started.

▪ What do we do? Choose a focus, a habit, something you want to change.

▪ Look through the book TOGETHER so you can see how the workbook will get you from your own "before" picture to your own "after."

I do hope to hear from you sometime on how it's going or to get started in your first call. Thank you for being here.

Contents

Practical Strategies: Your Playbook

Unlock the Window and Let in Fresh Air

Education about ADHD is validating. You'll learn what is normal for someone with ADHD. Learning about ADHD and *your* ADHD will begin to give you a new view on how to manage more easily.

Take A Glimpse Outside

Patterns are observations about your behavior. Noticing more about what has worked in the past gives you strategies to return to. And watching yourself gives you a focus, a place to start.

Really SEE What's Going on

To get better and good at anything in life, practice is the route to get there. Please try to have patience and self-compassion.

Inch That Window Open to A New View

"Small" wins feed motivation. Tracking small steps and progress along the way shows how much you *have* done instead of what's still not done. Look for the smallest signs of success at first! *Really small.*

Working Together

You are naturally creative, resourceful and a perfectly imperfect human being. We all are.

This playbook will be your companion, guiding, asking questions, and providing positive support for you throughout.

The answers and insights are ones you will find inside yourself.

Your answers are just for you. They are not weird, silly or here for anyone else's judgment.

Notice, observe, and reflect in a mindful, compassionate, nonjudgmental way towards yourself.

I know you can do it. You've taken a big first step!

You're Ready to Jump in, Right?

Because that's what ADHD can do to you, get you to jump right in, or make you so cautious, that you take a long time to get started.

You get hyper focused or are detached from others (are you paying attention to me?) and in your head. You lose track of why you started something or lose track of time. You might give up, backslide... and here comes the negative self-talk, beating up on yourself for not doing what you set out to do. It's a cycle.

Instead, you're going to sit on the grass you see out the window. We will increase your self-awareness and awareness of how ADHD shows up for you; it is unique to each person. A *new view* needs a new perspective and new strategies (along with a way to remember them since ADHD is in the mix).

This playbook will help you get from "here" to "there," whatever change you're making.

Don't Know Where to Start? Let's Sort it out Together.

Here are examples of 9 issues you could be wrestling with. I've also given you five starter questions to ask yourself, to sort out which issue rises to the top. That will be the one you work on first, using this playbook. You can always return again for the next issue, but you need a focus, right? If not, you're looking out that window, looking at EVERYthing and getting overwhelmed. But here, we want to take action and change things together.

Questions to ask yourself to figure out what to focus on or where to start.

- ❑ What frustrates you the most: Create your own issues "boxes" and put a # on each box.
- ❑ What frustrates others?
- ❑ What makes you feel like: This isn't who I am!
- ❑ What affects your home or work life the most?
- ❑ Finish this sentence for each issue: if I could solve this, it would mean that ....

If this still doesn't help you with focus, that's what your free call with me is for.
Sue@CoachSueWest.com or 603.765.9267 cell/text to set up a time to talk and get focused.

ADHD Sections for Your Playbook: How it All Fits

Let's get an overview of how this workbook/playbook will work to support you.

1 Unlock the Window and Let in Fresh Air

Rediscover some good stuff about yourself which will help you figure out how to support yourself this time AND maintain your habit or change. Many of us forget about these good things because ADHD can push them down so deep underneath the ways you don't believe in ourselves. You'll discover the strengths and superpowers you DO have. You'll also learn what is perfectly normal for someone with a brain which has ADHD (usually a relief!)

2 Take A Glimpse Outside

Where to start! Joining you will be your Change Chart. Focus on a small thing you want to change. You'll have examples. You'll use the same chart throughout the workbook as you add what you learn here You'll also look at time management a bit, because if it's new habit or routine you're starting (the most common use of the workbook), we have to look at WHEN you'll do that routine or habit. Figuring out the "when" for your new habit will increase your chances of really doing it this time. You'll look at when you have the most energy for the new habit or change, also to up your chances of some success with the habit. You'll also look at what's worked before and how it worked; we can usually find some good stuff in there to use again.

3 Really SEE What's Going on

You'll continue building your chart or worksheet. Now, you need some practice of this habit or change. To get better at anything, you need to take small steps and practice. You have to take the rope bridge to get from where you are now to where you want to be, a step at a time. Please try to have patience and self-compassion as you work through the practice. Keep track of what's happening.

4 Inch Open That Window to A New View

You'll read my ideas and advice about keeping track of your progress through "small wins." These will feed motivation to continue, like putting gas in a car. These will show you how much you *have done* instead of the ADHD default habit which is "What I didn't do." You'll also read about temporary setbacks or falling off the wagon and how to get back on, one of the biggest issues with ADHD. You're going to need (because of the ADHD) have to have safety net to make getting back to our habits easier.

Your Change Chart

- You'll focus on ONE small habit or a routine you want to build/change.

- You'll use the Change Chart throughout the workbook, adding to it.

- It's your way to keep track of what you're working on and how you do.

ADHD Playbook: Section 1

Unlock the Window

Take A Glimpse Outside

Really SEE What's Going

Inch Open That Window
to A New View

1 **Unlock the Window and Let in Fresh Air**

You'll work on awareness: (1) of how ADHD shows up in your days and (2) of some <u>good aspects</u> about yourself, which you may have forgotten about with the ADHD at work. That will help you with how to support yourself this time AND maintain your habit or change.

You forget about these good things because ADHD can push them down so deep that you may lose faith in yourself. You'll discover the strengths and superpowers you DO have. You'll also learn what is perfectly normal for someone with ADHD. It's not an excuse, but it will help you realize you're not alone. This *can* be managed.

Ever have this happen? You know what to do …. And then forget to do it, when the time arrives to do it. You walk in the grocery store, with just a few items in mind to buy. IN the grocery store, you forget. Your spouse asks you to do something after work and you've got it, solidly in mind when you have that conversation. Then something happens during the day, or your tired, or …. And you forget to follow through. Who's frustrated? Yes, both of you. ADHD affects you and all those around you. [Ask, if you're not sure that's true.]

The memory issues are normal. And solvable, in creative ways. Part of the deal with ADHD is that our memories are inherently not as strong as someone's without ADHD. It is part of our brain chemistry. It is *not* about intelligence. On the other hand, a fairly common ADHD strength is that people make connections among ideas and think bigger picture.

So, it's not really Attention Deficit. If it's fascinating, engaging, inspiring, interesting, creative …. attention and therefore memory of those experiences work fairly well. No deficit. More like an overabundance of attention and memory. They're connected. If it's boring, tedious tasks, there's less memory, less attention to these. Deficit, sure.

So what we want to do is even out some of the attention and memory. We want to 'externalize' the parts of your ADHD which are better managed not in your mind, but outside of it.

For example, as you work through whatever change you want, using this workbook, that's externalizing your work. This workbook **gives you one place to keep track**. You'll find education, tracking sheets, tips and motivational comments from others who have been where you are.

When you finally realize that it's been ADHD all along... Well, that explains a lot.

And then there's a time of looking back on your life, wondering "What if?" Education about ADHD is the best next step because you'll realize you're not the **only** one who does things the way you do. Or has memory issues. Or trouble prioritizing in your mind. You'll learn what is normal and common among people who have ADHD. As Rick Green of <u>TotallyADD.com</u> and the series <u>ADD and Loving It</u> says "Bend the world to you." And not the other way around, which is what most of us have always done!

As you go through this section, a window will begin to open up into how *you* do things. And when that happens, you can begin to figure out what to "do with" your ADHD. How to manage it, accept it as a unique part of you, and figure out what is unique.

These first exercises will remind you of your strengths, your values and what you stand for – all *positive* places to start from. Sometimes you need these reminders and especially when "nothing seems to work."

Education, too, will show you that your days *really can be easier, so let's start with a key concept about how the ADHD mind works differently.*

How "Executive Functions" Matter to Daily Life

Executive functions are at the heart of the challenges with ADHD. They're managed by the neural pathways, chemicals and across different parts of the brain. Dr. Thomas

Brown wrote an excellent, understandable and practical article, and also created this useful diagram*.

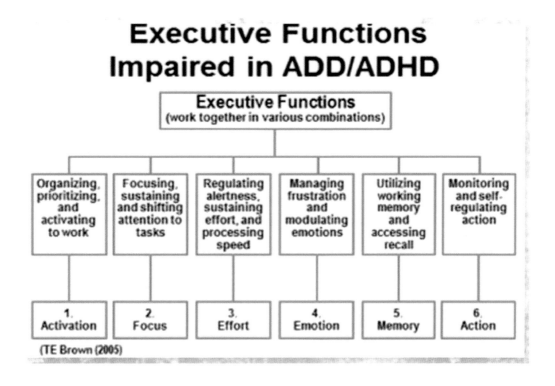

Here is an example of how executive functions play out in the daily, tiring struggle for someone with ADHD. I hope what you will see is that things like a morning routine ARE difficult, because of the reasons below. So if you're saying to yourself, that it "should be" easier, or someone in your family says it, this will help you explain "It's complicated."

Morning Routine

The pieces you need to juggle are: pictured below and writing or picture drawing work great to get all the puzzle pieces out in front of you so you can see the order more clearly.

- **17** pieces of the routine to order and organize!
- Ignoring distractions, filtering out what is not in your routine.
- Emotions – yours and everyone else's – keeping calm amidst some chaos.
- Switching gears. Wearing different hats during your morning then at work. Solution: map it out on paper or in your phone. Get it out in front of you.

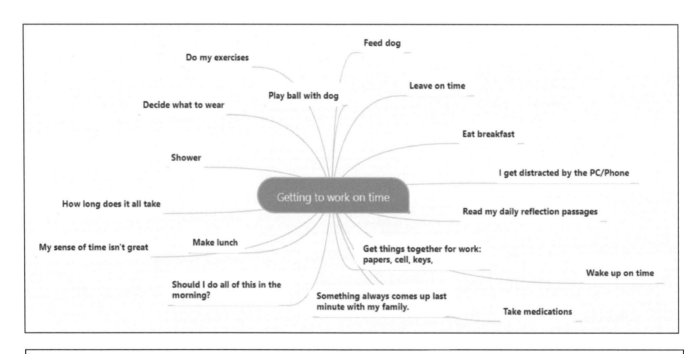

Mind map of "Getting to work on time," created by Sue West, using MindMeister.

Exercise: About Your ADHD

Your Diagnostic Report: "She is ADHD" is a way to reinforce that you're only identified by your ADHD, but that's old, negative thinking. You are <u>not</u> your ADHD; you are a person who *has* ADHD. Education will help you understand ADHD and what's normal.

Circle the kinds of education you've used to learn about ADHD [or search out each].

"How to ADHD" videos   Attention Talk Radio   Totally ADD   Additudemag.com
Blogs   Books   Podcasts   Webinars   CHADD: Children and Adults with ADHD
ADDA: Attention Deficit Disorder Association

What are you still curious about?

Focusing on one or two aspects at most, at a time, is the best way to go versus continually studying "all" of ADHD.

Get curious about <u>your own</u> ADHD and how it shows up in your daily life AND for those around you.

"Thinking of my life in chapters was not just helpful, but energizing, by way of getting me interested in new ways to think about how to design a life that fits for me, in a specific timeline."

How does your own version of ADHD show up in daily life? This will help you understand what to manage.

_____

_____

_____

Exercise: Your Diagnostic Report

If you've had an official assessment by a psychologist, psychiatrist or neuropsychologist, take out your report copy. Write down key points about how your ADHD shows up. This exercise will help you get to know *your ADHD; that's important because there are many symptoms and you'll need to know where to focus.*

Which "presentation(s)" of ADHD is yours? <u>(inattentive, hyperactive or combined?</u> <u>severe, moderate?)</u> And is it low/moderate/severe?

_____

Did you bring anyone with you and how was that useful?* What are your key symptoms (how does your ADHD show up?)

_____

_____

*A common issue with the ADHD brain is a lack of self-awareness, including how others are affected by the ADHD behavior. You focus so much energy managing the undiagnosed ADHD that your insight suffers; I ask this question because your self-awareness is part of this playbook. This is part of the ADHD neurological differences.

<u>Example:</u> I didn't realize it took asking me something "14 times" [at home] for me to remember to do it. Now, I have strategies to support my working memory, and including anxiety, which often is found with ADHD. Being asked multiple times is not fair to those around me, because *they* are not supposed to enable me. I am responsible

ADHD Strengths: Yes, ADHD Can Be Amazing!

Don't you always hear how difficult life is with ADHD? You talk to ourselves negatively. Your family and coworkers don't understand or may not even know you have it.

I've worked 10 years+ with people who have ADHD in a practical, coaching role. These are the *strengths* I've noticed. Does everyone have these? No. But … you have more than you probably realize or acknowledge. So watch for these in yourself.

1. Tremendous resilience: Many people have struggled, wondering why they failed at college, abused alcohol or drugs (often to mask ADHD symptoms). We keep on trying and we're still here!

2. Idea connectors: This connecting of things other people don't see is a superpower.

3. In the moment, and then not: This the upside of staying in the moment when your brain is fully engaged.

"I always thought being organized had to look a certain way—and that way never really fit me. This opened up new ways of getting organized that worked to my strengths. "

4. Belief in themselves [once acceptance and symptoms are managed well]: After the relief of "Oh, that's what's been hampering me all these years," there's the belief that *more is possible*. I often hear in a first call: *I know I have more potential. I know my life can be richer. I need strategies so I can live to my potential.*

5. Creative thinkers, and out of the box problem solvers. As some clients say, "My solutions may sound weird, funny or silly to others without ADHD, but they work for me!"

6. Curiosity. Curiosity keeps us more open to other's perspectives, to learning and to not judging.

7. In the moment. Yes, the now/not now phrase we've all heard. Also true that "in the moment" means we get more from the moment. We may not be calmly mindful, but we *are* in the moment.

8. Many remember impressions or rich stories, or how they *felt* about a person, event or situation. Details, not so much, but there are others around us who are great at this. We tend to be more conceptual and sometime bigger picture thinkers. How many CEO's have you read about who say they have ADHD?

9. Stick-to-itiveness. Being able to hyper focus on something is rewarding; you learn more; you solve a problem; you're not distracted. Moderation, as with everything, can be a strategy. Trying hard is the norm. Sometimes extra hard.

10. Sensitivity: Whether due to a life time of struggling to keep up, or because senses tend to be more alert, you'll find we are more attuned when we are engaged.

11. Risk taker – some.

12. Intelligent. I put this here because ADHD struggles make it hard to see someone's intelligence. Once they manage the symptoms, it all becomes quite clear.

Exercise: Explore Your Strengths

Many adults with ADHD have experienced years of failing to meet expectations of themselves. So it is easy to forget that we do have strengths.

Focus on what they are first. Eventually we'll figure out strategies to use your strengths more often instead of trying to "fix" the things we're not so good at.

What are your strengths? If you're feeling today like you don't have any/many, try this question instead.

What compliments do you hear from friends, colleagues, family or in performance reviews at work? Ask someone who knows you fairly well.

Whether you believe the answers or not yet, write down what you are told. This will become believable at some point. [If you want an online assessment, try the VIA Character Strengths one, from free to $$$.]

_____

_____

_____

Exercise: Values and Why They Matter

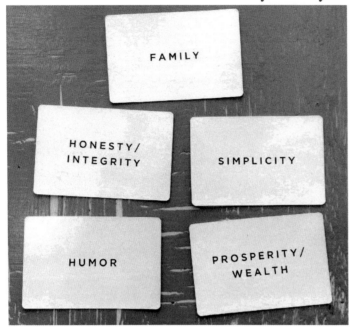

What is important to your core? What is most important in your life? What do you stand for?

Have you ever explored your *values?* Values show up in daily life when we make *choices* about how to use our time.

I promise: Values aren't just a nice theoretical exercise. If you have something you can't get yourself to do, reframing it as important to something you hold important – a value – gives you a different perspective, a different view of the task or chore. When you use your values this way, you'll find the motivation and momentum you were looking for!

For example, "Irene" was having trouble because the chores were overwhelming. Her children were 5,8, and 11. We reframed some of those chores as ways to teach her children important life skills they would need once on their own. We talked about involving others because she wanted to create an environment and a family culture. Both were key values.

For "Sarah," a value was having creativity in her life. It inspired her and helped her mind slow down, keeping a better work life balance for her. We realized that she had *none of the creativity* she needed in her life. Once we introduced that, and reorganized her days a bit, she felt more in balance, less stressed and calmer in general.

Exercise: Values

Instructions: Sort through these words on the next page and narrow your value choices to three. Start with this list and add your own if you'd like. Definitions are up to you.

If three words does not seem possible, then group together similar words. As you think about it more, you may find one of the words in a group stands above the rest. Or you may find a new word that reflects what you wanted to say for a whole group of words.

Your *experience* with this exercise is interesting. It is meant to take some time. I've included questions below, for reflection.

Accountability	Faith	Resourcefulness
Accuracy	Family	Responsiveness
Achievement	Flexibility	Self-reliance
Adventure	Forgiveness	Service
Affection	Freedom	Simplicity
Autonomy	Friendship	Speed
Calm	Goodness	Strength
Challenge	Gratitude	Tolerance
Change	Harmony	Tradition
Cleanliness	Honesty	Tranquility
Collaboration	Honor	Trust
Commitment	Humor	Truth
Communication	Improvement	Variety
Community	Independence	Wisdom
Competence	Individuality	
Cooperation	Integrity	
Coordination	Justice	
Courage	Knowledge	
Courtesy	Leadership	
Creativity	Loyalty	
Decisiveness	Obedience	
Democracy	Openness	
Discipline	Personal Growth	
Discovery	Practicality	
Diversity	Privacy	
Efficiency	Progress	
Equality	Punctuality	
Excellence	Reason	
Fairness	Reliability	

Reflection Questions:

1. What was difficult about this exercise? What was easier?

2. Did anything surprise you?

3. How did you *feel* about the results?

4. How have your values changed over the years?

5. Notice anything about inner-directed values (self) and outer-directed (towards others)?

6. How are you aligning daily life and time choices with your values and needs?

Remembering these important values and strengths: On the next page is a page you may want to copy or tear out and post where you can see it often as a reminder.

My choices reflect what I value.

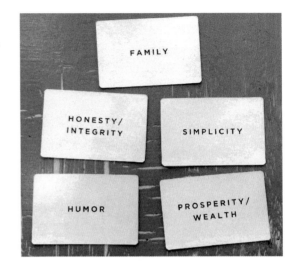

My most important values are:

1. _____

2. _____

3. _____

And my strengths are:

1. _____

2. _____

3. _____

Please post or take a photo on your phone as a reminder.

ADHD Playbook: Section 2

2 Take A Glimpse Outside

Ready to start? Joining will be your **Change Chart.** Here's what is ahead:

- You'll focus on ONE small thing you want to add or change.
- You'll update the Change Chart throughout the workbook as you add to it.
- We'll look at 4 aspects of your life which increase your chances of success.
  - ○ Time: When could you create time for this?
  - ○ Energy: When do you have the energy (Or times you don't!)
  - ○ Attention: When is your focus the best for this type of habit?
  - ○ Past successes: What's worked before and how did you do that? We can usually find some good ideas to use again.
  - ○ Remembering to do what you want, when you want to.

Patterns

Get to know your ADHD like a friend and you'll find it MUCH easier to manage it. When you are more aware of how your version of ADHD shows up each day, then it's easier to pinpoint where to start. A welcome relief, knowing where to start, right?!

Identifying what's working will give you best practices to return to – things you <u>know</u> work for you. And noticing what doesn't work as well, or when you're "off your game" will identify areas or habits to focus on so you can create – or bring back – strategies that will work.

A second step will be to figure out how to *remember what works*, because ADHD needs memory supports. A client said: "I call my calendar, phone and notebook (to do lists) my 'external brain.' I feel as if it opens up space in my mind to think creatively, or feel less on the go, more reflective and I get so much more started, finished and done!"

 I call the "remember what works" piece your *safety net*. By that, I mean: you will know what works, but your brain with ADHD has a working memory issue. So you'll need ways remember what works so you consistently use these strategies. That's typically the key piece missing when I work with clients. *I know what to do; I'm not doing it.*

Exercise: Before and After

Now that you've focused on yourself and how your ADHD shows up, we're going to start with the one change you wanted to focus on. Get that going and solid as a habit, then move onto something else. Give yourself about 3 months to instill a new habit – to make it automatic. If it takes longer, that's perfectly normal for someone who has ADHD or for anyone with big life events happening.

An example of the Change Chart with a focused issue starts on the next page. You'll see a "before" picture and the "after" picture of how this client wanted things to be.

Daniel Goleman, in "The Power of Positive Planning" notes that research proves that positive pictures or visions of goals will motivate us. In fact, the more senses we use to describe the "after" picture, the clearer the future becomes (2014).

"Talking about positive goals activates brain centers that open you up to new possibilities. But if you change the conversation to what you should do to fix yourself, it closes you down,"

Richard Boyatzis, psychologist at the Weatherhead School of Management at Case Western

Attaching *meaning* through those last two questions can be a motivator because it connects to your values. It's not an "I should" but "I want to because of this deeply held belief or meaning." It's not magic, but it is a core piece of this framework, and something you'll return to often.

Before picture: I'm frequently late…. or rushing so I'm not late. When I've rushed, then I'm not present and I miss important points in a meeting or a phone call. And then I have to find out what I missed, which takes up more time. I don't feel like I'm a contributing member of the team. And my manager sat me down recently talk about all of this. All around, I don't feel like a great employee nor a great spouse and parent.

After picture: I'd show up to meetings and appointments on time. I'd have everything I need with me. I'd feel totally present and ready to add what I *know* are good ideas and solutions at our meetings.

If I could solve this, then I would have time for: Well, I'd have more energy at night to spend with our kids. I'd be able to do more around the house. Eventually, maybe I could get back to school, which is a dream, to change careers. If I weren't tied up with catching up at work on Saturdays, we could have more fun or I could take a class or something that I want to do. And not feel guilty!

How would this be important in my work or life? All around, I would feel I'm doing my best, and really am being the good employee, spouse and parent I know I can be. I'm not being the person I can be proud of these days, always in crisis and not being there for people, or role modeling for my kids.

Now, let's start your own chart. Start with the first two rows, before and after.

Before	
After	
What made it work in the past?	
Who or what resources could you use as a safety net?	
How will you remember to practice this new habit or strategy?	
What is a "small win?"	
	**I would like you to skip to section 4 and read what "small win" looks like and means. You'll return later, but it'll help as you set up this chart. Hint: Usually "small" needs to be smaller!

Exercise: What's Worked before

I've often found that in a client's past are some strategies which *sort of* worked, but did work yet the client stopped using them or changed strategies. Or there are some which worked great and need to be brought back. One of the problems with ADHD is that when you are not paying attention, it's impossible to remember something (because nothing registers in your brain). we find that a strategy that used to work can be used again or can be modified to work again. And *this time* we also need to figure out how to remind ourselves to try the new habit and keep trying; that's a key for people with ADHD, having that safety net.

"Getting unstuck is what I needed."

Think about your one area you want to change: think about a time in your life when you had this better under control.

When was that?

_____

When did you have things better under control; how did you do that?

_____

How did you start the habit? And remember to use it?

_____

What have you already tried to manage your ADHD symptoms and especially the one thing you want to focus on?

When do you know you're "on your game?" How do you know? What are the signs: body, mind, feelings, instincts?

_____

_____

_____

....and "Off your game?" What happened to cause you to stop using a strategy, habit or routine something that used to work for you?

_____

_____

Examples of Strategies

Below are a few common issues clients wrestle with and some "starter" strategies for you. Look for the topic or habit you're working on and see what you might try out.

Project Work

Use a timer to focus and to get a sense of time: Start the timer at the beginning of your project for 30 minutes. When it goes off, sit back in your chair. Check where you are. Are you focused where you wanted to be? How long did the time "feel" like? People with ADHD have a sense of time, believe it or not. It's different though from what is considered the "norm." Is this a regular project? If so, keep track of how long it took. That'll help you next time with estimates.

Double your estimated time, if you have no idea how long something will take. Clients often say they underestimate time. The easiest way to start learning how long things take is to double the estimate you come up with. Keep track of estimated and actual for a few projects and you'll see how far off you are and can tailor the "doubling." Might be more or could be less. Or depending on the size of the project.

Breakup big projects into small steps or "tiny tasks. "START with your end date. Work backwards from that date. Fill in any date you do know. Start in the middle of the timeframe, if that's a date you know. Use post it notes, mind mapping or a sketch to write down all the steps *first. And then order them.* Two separate steps. Don't try to do both at once; that's an example of executive function, where seeing the steps out in front of you, visually, is one process; the second one is to decide on the order. Many people without ADHD can order things in their minds; in my experience with people who have ADHD, this is easier, less tiring and more satisfying as a 2-step process.

Ways to Hold Yourself "Accountable"

"Accountable" is typically a negative word. People call and want accountability. It's usually because they don't believe they can follow through on their own so they NEED accountability. To some degree, we all do, but I'd like you to understand that you *can* hold yourself to what you say you'll do. [Some starter strategies are below.]. What I learned at Coach Approach for Organizers ten years ago now, was to add the word "curious" to "accountability." Curious accountability is compassionate, nonjudgmental and we are trying to discover what happened, whether a strategy worked, sort of worked, or not at all. Usually, we're in the "sort of/sometimes" category at first. I often say doing something more than zero times is an example of a starter, small win. And we go on from there. At least you STARTED. Otherwise, you'll beat up on yourself for not doing it 7 days out of 7, and that's flat out unrealistic for all of us, especially with ADHD and especially starting a new habit.

So it's "curious accountability."

Race the timer. It can put a little bit of pressure which gets many people going.

Accountability partner: This can be a weekly phone call. It can be your teenager who does homework while you do your work in the same room.

Do things with others a/k/a don't do it alone. Some people are extraverted or need the energy of people to get things done. Work in teams. Call someone while you work. Facetime or Skype/Zoom together.

Body double: This is a person who works alongside you, and may or not physically help with your task. Their value is that this your anchor of energy. Try it to understand.

Instrumental music: Play quiet music, no words to sing along to, as you work on something. This can keep you focused and also act as white noise around you.

Total quiet around you or people? Know which works better for you when you need to focus. I've often worked with people who can't work or do homework at home; they need an offsite office, a coffee shop or a library. It's the environment and it's also: *I am here to do xyz.* A commitment to yourself.

Start a day with meditation or other quiet forms of sitting. It starts your day with a practice of focus and a quiet mind.

Podcasts/audio while working on a tedious task, and only those which require little thinking! [Filing, sometimes organizing, dusting and vacuuming].

Use Reminders to Support your ADHD Memory

Reminders are an example of a "safety net." If you don't remember, these will help.

Reminders: Use only for key reminders, not everything or they aren't effective.

Keep hitting "snooze" until you are *actually* doing the task you wanted to be reminded of, and do not hit "Dismiss." Because it'll be dismissed from your memory, too.

Sometimes people need a reminder before the reminder. For example, setting a reminder 10 minutes before you need to leave often pushes people to "do one more thing," and then they are late. To "wake" your mind and shift gears more easily, try setting a reminder 20 minutes and then also 10 minutes ahead; you'll have to play with what gets you to move.

Visual reminders: My dad used to toss something on the floor to remind himself.

Use post-it notes or index cards as visual reminders of the day's 3 top priorities to keep them in front of you.

Use a post-it note to write out your morning routines steps with times, so you get out the door on time. Work backwards.

Lists – ADHD style.

Lists get lost. Gather in a notebook instead and *label the front.*

Use more digital than paper, but be careful of getting "lost in your pc/phone/tablet." Lists online are easily shared, too, though, so it's easy to enlist others. Try a hybrid of using digital to hold the list and print out your list for the day so it's visible.

Create a daily roadmap of things to do, out of your big, master, laundry list of all things. Start with 3 tasks. Add more if you do those.

Don't be afraid that you "shouldn't" use colored pens, patterned folders, and other colorful ways to spruce up your notebook, bullet journal or whatever you use.

Create a "don't pay attention" list. Or a "keep out of sight" list. Delete or move apps off your home screen if they distract you.

Self-care for a calmer mind

Journaling or morning pages clear your mind so you start the day fresh.

Choose a fairly consistent wakeup time and sleep time. That will help you with sleep but also with a better sense of the time during the days.

Exercise and meditation: both proven techniques for focus and improved ability to filter out distractions.

Routines: morning/midday/eve. Group together or link together tasks which naturally seem to go together in your mind. It's much easier to write down or remember one routine than 5 or 6 little tasks.

Keep a journal or a tracking mechanism for mental and physical health so you can hold yourself accountable. [I use HabitNest journals.]

Now, continue filling in your chart. You just read about starter strategies. You also thought about strategies which have worked for you in the past.

Susan Fay West
Fill in lines 3, 4 and 5 as best you can.

Before	
After	
What made it work in the past?	
How will you remember to practice this new habit or strategy?	
What is a "small win?"	
Who or what resources could you use as a safety net?	

Organizing Your Days: Managing Time, Energy and Attention

You might recognize this as:

- being drained at the end of the day [no matter your age];
- last minuteitis [just one more thing to work on before I leave];
- looking up and the whole day has gone by …. very fast;
- difficulty prioritizing;
- frequently late…. or rushing so you're not late;
- letting other people take up too much of your time.

Now, we will look at your time, energy and attention throughout the day. We need to figure out: WHEN will you work on this habit and WHAT else is getting in your way of being consistent with the habit. Usual culprits are a disorganized day, trying out the habit at the worst possible time of day for your energy/ADHD rhythms, or poor self-care, which is a critical part of taking care of your ADHD.

Exercise: Unravel Your Time Challenges

The wheel <u>on the next page</u> helps you figure out where to start tackling your time challenges. Mark each slice from 0-10, rating your satisfaction. Remember that this is a time to be realistic, not to beat yourself up for every little thing that didn't go perfectly right. Everything that doesn't go as expected is an opportunity to learn.

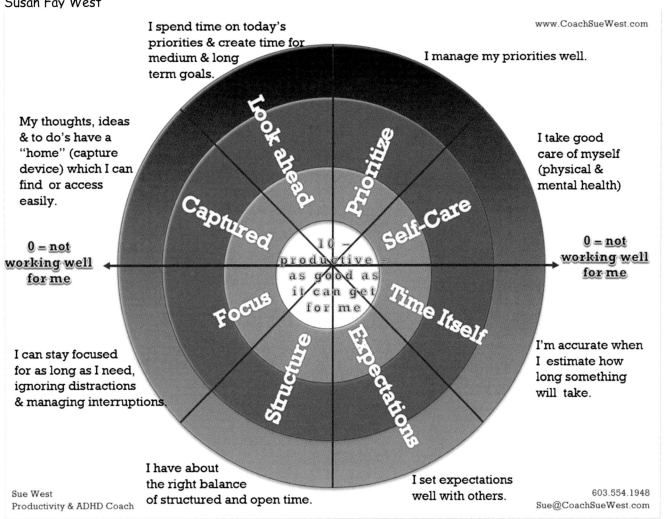

I spend time on today's priorities & create time for medium & long term goals.

www.CoachSueWest.com

I manage my priorities well.

My thoughts, ideas & to do's have a "home" (capture device) which I can find or access easily.

I take good care of myself (physical & mental health)

0 = not working well for me

0 = not working well for me

Look ahead

Prioritize

Captured

Self-Care

10 – productive – as good as it can get for me

Focus

Time Itself

Structure

Expectations

I can stay focused for as long as I need, ignoring distractions & managing interruptions.

I'm accurate when I estimate how long something will take.

I have about the right balance of structured and open time.

I set expectations well with others.

Sue West
Productivity & ADHD Coach

603.554.1948
Sue@CoachSueWest.com

Exercise: Your Time Choices

Now what? The first column has a slice of the pie or wheel you just completed.

From the wheel	What's working?	What's not working?	What would you like?
I manage my priorities well.			
I take good care of my physical and mental health.			
I set expectations well with others.			
I'm accurate when I estimate how long something will take			
I have about the right balance of structured and open time.			
I can stay focused for as long as I need ignoring distractions and managing interruptions.			
My thoughts and ideas have a "home" [capture device] which I can find or access easily.			
I spend time on today's priorities and create time for medium and long term goals.			

Exercise: Self-Care: Critical for ADHD Health

Why is this <u>extra</u> important to people with ADHD? A couple of reasons:

#1 We get mentally tired just keeping our minds, days, tasks, activities organized. It is part of the executive function differences of ADHD, so we learn different strategies to manage this.

#2 Your ADHD is more in control when you don't practice self-care. When you're tired, physically or mentally, it's much harder to keep using your best practice strategies, which help you manage your ADHD symptoms.

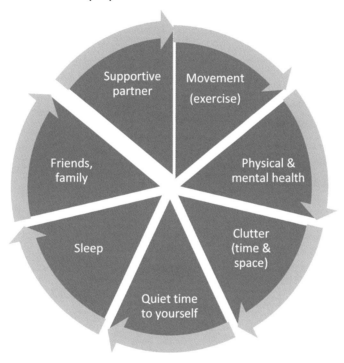

#3 Self-care can include medication, but it does not have to for everyone. An excellent book on Alternative Strategies by Dr. Stephanie Sarkis, Natural Relief for Adult ADHD.

#4 You may be more inclined towards emotional impulsivity and other symptoms which are directly affected by fatigue.

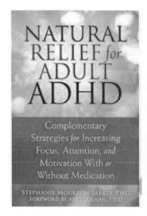

And you'll see more reasons in the exercise about self-care. Think about physical *and* mental health as adding up to taking care of yourself.

Step one is to break it down into small parts like on the wheel. You'll always find a focus and a solution if you dive into the details. You can use the wheel [next page] and the chart just after it to figure out where you are and what you want.

Self-Care Wheel Instructions

You know how a smooth car ride needs all tires working at their best pressure levels? Same thing here. If one or more of your self-care pieces is ranked lower, it's like a lopsided tire. And then that is where you would focus first typically.

Mark how you feel how things are going. Try to use the numbers _between_ zero and 10, not only the zero or the 10. Focus on what you appreciate or are grateful for. This will help you figure out where to focus first. It will also demonstrate your progress, when you make changes, and then use the wheel again.

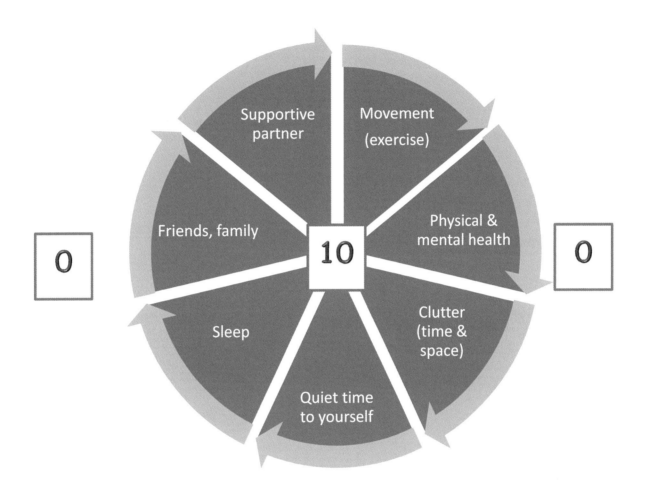

Exercise: Self-Care Choices

Where you are now, what's working or not, and where you're trying to get to.

Self-Care Aspect	What's working?	What's not working?	What would you like?
Sleep: getting to sleep "on time;" staying asleep; waking up			
Supportive family.			
Supportive life partner.			
Movement, exercise			
Stress management			
Physical health			
Medication management			
Boundaries: at work, at home. How well do you respect yours?			
Managing your mental health.			
Clutter: Your home and work spaces.			
Keeping up with household responsibilities (rituals,			

routines, systems, presence)			
Time for yourself.			

Exercise: Daily Attention, Focus and Energy Rhythms

This exercise I'd like you to do for at least a few days; a week is even better because you'll see week vs. weekend differences. It's hard to switch gears sometimes.

The purpose of this is to:

- figure out when your most focused, productive time is so you can protect it;

- understand what gets in your way; how can you protect it more?

- when is your attention and focus best?

- help with sleep patterns and what's getting in the way;

- to help even out energy levels of your days, so you're not exhausted at the end of the day (personal time!)

- to see what you have not made time for OR are forgetting (meals are common)

Starts on the next page.

Changing Habits; ADHD Style

	Monday	Tuesday	Wednesday	Thursday	Friday	Saturday	Sunday
Morning segment							
Wakeup time. Consistency is best.							
ADHD medication time							
Morning energy level: low/med/hi							
Ability to focus?							
Exercise/movement time and how much did you do?							
Midday segment							
Lunch time. Meals and breaks refresh and reset.							
Meds time							
Energy level, ability to focus.							

End of day segment	Monday	Tuesday	Wednesday	Thursday	Friday	Saturday	Sunday
Usual dinner time							
Usual meds time							
Energy level and/or ability to focus							
About when does your wind down routine begin?							
Usual bedtime? Sleep issues? Number of hours?							

What are your patterns? What did you notice?

What might you rearrange or do differently?

_____

_____

_____

ADHD Playbook: Section 3

Unlock the Window

Take A Glimpse Outside

Really SEE What's Going on

Inch Open That Window to A New View

3 Really See What's Going on

- Time to practice and learn to really see what's going on.
  - You'll have general advice from me on practicing a new habit;
  - You'll read 3 client examples – their change charts;
  - And complete yours;
  - Learn from practice! Be curious.

Practice

We'll continue building your chart with practicing this new habit or routine. To get better at anything, we need to take small steps and practice.

Please try to have patience and self-compassion as you work through the practice. Keep track of what's happening.

You're going to focus on one brick in the wall of the building. Not the building nor even the whole wall.

Stay in the present and focused on the one thing you're attempting to change.

Some ideas that work for various people: setting an intention, declaring it to yourself or others so your ADHD mind gets engaged, deciding how you'll get yourself to remember to try this new habit, and thinking about the kind of accountability, oversight or support you need to keep it going.

General Advice for Practicing a New Habit

- One key point is not to expect perfection. If you succeed once, that's more than zero and that's progress. If something else happens, you will learn from that, too. Like the saying that we learn best from mistakes, right?

- Take notes on what works and doesn't work so you can *learn from* your practice. Use the chart or a notes app.
- The point is to slow down, observe yourself and learn from doing … or what you're not doing.
- Give it time. You've perhaps heard a habit takes 21 days? Not true it turns out, with more recent research. And it will take *longer* for someone with ADHD *because* of what's going on in your brain. This is one reason that strategies as well as a Plan B are important.
- Use your alarms, reminders and prompts to support your practice. This is like wearing glasses for eyesight differences, so this is about acceptance of your ADHD, too.
- Co-workers and family typically will not notice your progress as soon as you do.
- Tell an accountability partner what you plan to do. Choose someone who already believes in your abilities to make this change, **not** someone who has heard it "many times before."

Exercise: Practice and Learn

Let's pull the work together and figure out how you'll remember to practice new habits and track progress. Here are a few clients' examples of how to do this. As you work, return to your Strengths and Values. Where do you see them showing up in what has worked for you in the past? Or how you could remember to practice? Because where is the motivation but in your values and using your strengths.

	Client Example #1
Before	I constantly forget to bring things with me that I need - like to a work meeting or a friend's house or to an appointment. Then I have to return to get these things which makes me late or I rush and then I don't listen as well so I miss out. I feel like I'm fumbling all the time.
After	I'd show up with what I need, when I need it and look much more like a put together human being. I'd pay better attention to work meetings, to friendships, to my kids!
What made it work in the past?	When this happened in my first job, I would use sticky notes. I'd write out what I needed to remember and post it right on the door or right on my planner.
How will you remember to practice this new habit or strategy?	I could use sticky notes. I could also use calendar alerts, so when I set up a meeting, right in the calendar entry, I could add what I need to bring with me. I could also have a certain place where I put things as I realize I need them. Sort of like when I pack for vacation, I open the suitcase, and leave it open, dropping things in there right when I think of them.
Who or what resources could you use as a safety net?	I would do this at night and if by any chance I ran out of time, I'd have the morning as my safety net. But I'd set an earlier alarm, maybe 10 minutes different. And a reminder would help.

	Client Example #2
Before	I'm frequently late with work assignments or staying up way too late and working weekends to get them done. My manager has noticed and I've been spoken to. I know the material and have great ideas, but organizing them is so difficult. Then when I stay up late, I don't sleep well and begin this bad cycle which affects everything.
After	My work would be on time. I'd get the promotion I'm looking for. My manager would be confident in me again as would my clients. My family life will be a whole lot calmer, too. All around, I'd feel like a great employee and a great spouse and parent.
What made it work in the past?	In college, I had the same issue, staying up until midnight and beyond to get my school work done for the next day. Finally, I figured out that I could use index cards to organize my ideas, and then move them around to create the outline for my paper. When I would write, it was faster and easier to write; I followed the outline!
How will you remember to practice this?	With work projects, I could use index cards, post it notes or even a mind mapping tool. How would I remember? Well, because know it worked before, that's motivating to try it again. And I could write down "try index cards" right on my work task list as another reminder.
Who or what resources could you use as a safety net?	The mind mapping would actually be fun so I will try the index cards, knowing my new tech way might be more fun. If I set up a special space for all these materials, if would feel more official and like I was taking myself seriously. That emotion would be a strong safety net.

	Client Example #3
Before	I am overwhelmed with everything there is to do. My thoughts and ideas do not have a "home" [capture device]. I keep it all in my head and everything seems to get bigger as it moves around in my mind. When I've used a notebook, I could not find it. When I've used other tools, I use them, then stop. So I can't trust myself that I'll use any tool. So I use nothing.
After	I would have one place where everything would go. Every day, I'd look at the list, figure out what was priority and make up my roadmap for the day to follow. I'd feel accomplished, far less stressed and I actually think I would get more done without all the stress.
What made it work in the past?	There was one time when I used a colored notebook, with colored pens. It was very creative and I loved writing in it. I think that made it easier to *want* to use it. I'd look at it every night before I left work, figure out what the next day would be, and closed the book on today. It felt great!
How will you remember to practice this new habit or strategy?	I need to stop using so much technology and return to a beautiful, creative, colorful planner. I'll be able to see everything out at once on the pages by week. I'll want to use it because it's so beautiful. Oh, and I'm going to look up bullet journals because I think the creativity might work great! Off to Pinterest to find bullet journal info!
Who or what resources could you use as a safety net?	I'm going to ask someone I trust to be my accountability partner. I'll decide by what date I want to have the planner and by saying it aloud, that *intention* is strong enough for me. I also want to figure out which technology I'll stop using and tell my partner that. Delete it, hide it; somehow put blinders on.

Now, continue filling in your chart.

Before	
After	
What made it work in the past?	
How will you remember to practice this new habit or strategy?	
Who or what resources could you use as a safety net?	

ADHD Playbook: Section 4

4 Inch Open That Window to A New View

- A small win is a big deal. One small win will give you confidence that change is possible, a new view or perspective for you.
    - Practice and keep track of small wins.
    - Read the examples of our 3 clients' small wins.
    - Take the wisdom and advice here.
    - Keep track of what you learn when things do and do not work on a particular day. And get curious, not judgmental.

4 Inch Open That Window to A New View

I'll give ideas and advice about keeping track of your progress through "small wins." These will feed motivation to continue, like putting gas in a car. These will show you how much you *have done* instead of the ADHD default habit which is "What I didn't do." You'll also read about temporary setbacks or falling off the wagon and how to get back on, one of the biggest issues with ADHD. We always have to have safety net to make getting back to our habits easier.

Always remember: You will learn either because you **did** what you said you'd do ...at least a few times that week. You'll ALSO learn what got in the way (what you **did not** do). And then that can be solved, so it's not a recurring issue.

The smallest step forward IS progress. "Small" wins feed motivation and are like gas in the car you're wanting to move forward. Notice the smallest of improvements. You are human, so perfection is never the goal; we are headed a step up from where you are, one step. Some clients call it "moving the needle" or they look at it like earning karate belts, one level achieved and now practice for the next.

Small Win Examples

You have opened and read through the mail <u>three times this week</u>, where before, you opened it about every ten days or so. Bills are paid on time now.

You've been <u>late only twice in the past two weeks</u>, instead of almost daily like before.

You're pretty consistent about using your phone to keep a list of important things to remember. Before, your partner, spouse or manager would either have to remind you constantly or you'd forget a lot.

Many people think *they know* how well they are doing. Think about it though: ADHD is partly an attention and a memory issue. Many people I talk with start out saying they aren't doing well at all with their new habit. Yet when we dive into the details and ask more questions, they've done more than they realized.

<u>Again, please remember:</u> You will learn either because you **did** what you said you'd do ...at least a few times that week. You'll ALSO learn what got in the way (what you **did not** do). And then that can be solved, so it's not a recurring issue.

Let's add a column to the chart for tracking. Paper is much more visible than tracking on your phone. In sight and in mind!

Exercise: Strategies that Work

#1 Before	I constantly forget to bring things with me that I need - like to a work meeting or a friend's house or to an appointment. Then I have to return to get these things which makes me late or I rush and then I don't listen as well so I miss out. I feel like I'm fumbling all the time.
After	I'd show up with what I need, when I need it and look much more like a put together human being. I'd pay better attention to work meetings, to friendships, to my kids!
How will you track your progress?	I will notice when I am on time and mark it in my calendar/planner. I will see at the end of the week how I did.

#2 Before	I'm frequently late with work assignments or staying up way too late and working weekends to get them done. My manager has noticed and I've been spoken to. I know the material and I have great ideas, but organizing them is so difficult. Then when I stay up late, I don't sleep well and begin this bad cycle which affects everything.
After	My work would be on time. I'd get the promotion I'm looking for. My manager would be confident in me again as would my clients. My family life will be a whole lot calmer, too. All around, I'd feel like a great employee and a great spouse and parent.
How will you track your progress?	I can keep track of my bedtime on the self-care chart, or in a notebook I keep at my bed. And how many work projects I'm turning in on time: I could mark that on my calendar at work.

#3 Before	I am overwhelmed with everything there is to do. My thoughts and ideas do *not* have a "home" [capture device]. I keep it all in my head and everything seems to get bigger as it moves around and around in my mind. When I've used a notebook, I could not find it. When I've used other tools, I use them, then stop. So then I can't trust myself that I'll use any tool. So I use nothing.
After	I would have one place where everything would go. Every day, I'd look at the list, figure out what was priority and make up my roadmap for the day to follow. I'd feel accomplished, far less stressed and I actually think I would get more done without all the stress.
How will you track your progress?	I'd get it in play over the weekend and ready for Monday at work. I'd keep it one of two places: the kitchen table and then at work, open at my desk. If I can keep it where I'll see it and it's beautiful, I will use it. So the more writing I see, the better off I'll be, in a sense.

And now yours!

Before	
After	
What made it work in the past?	
How will you remember to practice this new habit or strategy?	
How will you track your progress?	
What's a small win?	

Temporary Setbacks: They Will Happen!

Solid systems are not just a "nice to have" productivity tool. They give us a foundation to push us back on track when we fall. They help us recover faster. Like a safety net. Or if you're the egg then systems are your nest, surrounding you so you don't fall again.

And when we have a crisis or some kind of setback and we forget to use our systems, that's okay. It happens. The point is how fast we recover. The point is NOT to do things perfectly right the first time.

When you go out to eat and your meal isn't right, **but** they do an excellent job making it right somehow, how does that feel? You've been HEARD. It also means that you are likely to give the restaurant a second chance.

They have an approach, standards, and a system. A system to *recover from a glitch.*

When I've said this about recovery, a light bulb goes on for the client I'm working with. I hear it time and again. Your plan B and your systems help you to recover quickly. You're giving yourself a second chance, which you deserve!!

"Any kind of accountability-like this workbook! - is extra helpful because it allows me to see how what I have done is beneficial to me. I don't automatically think of progress!"

Susan Fay West

My Example and My Strategies

This is my story as an example of how to get back on the wagon when I'd fallen off on exercising.

I have never been particularly athletic. I've had times when I've consistently gone to the gym or exercised on my own. Being the "right" weight was what I thought was important. And that was the problem. That, and thinking I had to be rigid about my schedule for exercise.

Sometime around one of my "big" birthdays, I figured out that exercise was about improving my health, energy and mental health. Age was part of it; I won't deny it! Although I was born with terrific health and wellness genes, I began to feel as if my luck might wear out as I got older. I'd been fortunate but maybe I'd better start doing something.

Back on the Wagon Approach: What works for me

I give myself permission to slow down or stop when life crises hit. Not work crises, but personal life events. I do realize that exercising relieves stress. The other part of my mind takes over though and I stop the exercise; there's not enough time! So I let it go, and give myself *permission* to do whatever feels comfortable, knowing I will ease back into it. Because adding one more thing to my list would cause my head (and heart) to explode.

I ease into it. As the crisis passes, I begin to set an intention to return to exercise. This time, I began by wearing my indoor biking outfit to work [in my home office]. And then one day that week, I took a spin on the bike in the middle of the day just for 5 or 10 minutes. I knew it would remind me of how it felt to be in better shape and have more energy. By the next week, I was doing my regular ½ hour and the following week, I was back up to 5 times a week.

Values motivate: I am a person who always thinks about the value of a purchase. When I went to the gym, I'd figure out a per visit fee based on the monthly fee as a motivator. When we considered getting rid of the expensive inside bike, I found it motivating to consider the wasted money and it helped get me back to biking. Frugality is a value for me, so it's a piece of the motivation. I LOVE to read and rarely have time for it. So I leave one or two books to my bike riding time; I only listen/read them when I'm on the bike. So I'm not really exercising! I "get to read" while I bike.

I plan it into my days. If I don`t plan for it, it doesn`t become a habit and it's too easy to stop. I also need a *weekend* plan because my schedule is different. Or on a day when I have a night meeting, I see it in my calendar which helps me make a plan B instead of skipping my usual biking time. I use my HabitNest journal and complete that each night, too – setting my intentions.

I keep exercise top of mind. How can you keep this in front of yourself? For me, I create a calendar reminder so it's visible. I added "biking progress" to my business accountability partner meetings! Also, I use various events as deadlines or mini goals, such as a conference, change of seasons, or a new outfit. I keep my clothes on my nightstand so they are the first thing I see, and a visible reminder. I have a whiteboard facing me where I do my exercises and biking, so I can chug right through them. And I use a small notebook to keep track, which I do before leaving the exercise space. Nothing like a notebook to hold you accountable.

Exercise: Bouncing Back

Think about a time in your life when you've stopped doing something, fallen off the wagon, or couldn't keep up with a habit … and then got yourself back to it. Reflect on how you did that, like my example above.

Write down your ways to get back on track here:

_____

_____

Where could you keep these best practices as reminders? In what form?
_____

_____

When times get tough, you'll have this list to *pull you* back onto the rails because it'll remind you of what works! And then you can take a step at a time and you'll be on your way.

Here we are at the end …. and at a new beginning.

My hope for you is that you have found hope, a roadmap and a new way to help yourself manage your ADHD symptoms.

The window has been opened.

The direction is there. You've learned a lot about yourself by now. It's up to you to take all of this and create your new perspective of life with ADHD.

Need oversight, accountability, coaching or support:

www.CoachSueWest.com 603.765.9267 cell/text

55461813R10042

Made in the USA
San Bernardino,
CA